At the Fair

Alison Hawes

Illustrated by Kay Widdowson

OXFORD

UNIVERSITY PRESS

A big fair came to town.

Everyone went to the fair.
There was lots to see.

Everyone went on the little rides.

"Come on the big rides,"
said Little Dragon.
Everyone looked at the big rides.

"Come on the big wheel,"
said Little Dragon.

Everyone went on the big wheel.

Not everyone liked it!

"Come on the big dipper,"
said Little Dragon.
Everyone went on the big dipper.

Not everyone liked it!

"Come on the ghost train,"
said Little Dragon.
Everyone went on the ghost train.

Not everyone liked it!

Everyone had a go on the hoopla
but not everyone got a prize.

Everyone had some candyfloss.
Everyone liked it.

It was time to go home.

Little Dragon didn't like it!